Do This In Remembrance of Me

LIVING THE EXAMPLE OF JESUS

Rev. Seamus P. Doyle

Lisa

God's blessing on your Journey.

+ Seamus

Liguori
ONE LIGUORI DRI
LIGUORI MO 6305

Imprimi Potest:
Richard Thibodeau, C.Ss.R.
Provincial, Denver Province
The Redemptorists

ISBN 0-7648-0972-5
Library of Congress Catalog Number: 2002108170

To order, call 1-800-325-9521
www.liguori.org
www.catholicbooksonline.com

Contents

At some point we can draw a line under the sufferings of our past; they are finished. We can lift our eyes to the future, and in the midst of suffering we can sense the beginning of something new. New seed sprouts in the scorched earth, new shoots and stalks push upward, and life unfolds toward the future. It is our same old life, not completely different, and yet in the space created by hope and confidence we become new people, no longer subject to fear, helplessness, and despair, but open to hope, capable of happiness, ripe for joy.

EUGENE DREWERMANN[1]

Home is where our roots are, the source from which our life has sprung. Sacred and emotional, there is something real that binds us closely to the place we call home. Come home, come home. This is the call of Christ, the call of love to the unloved to come home to ourselves to be healed, to have wholeness restored in us. Like the Prodigal, we go out in quest of fulfillment, sought on many levels; but fulfillment is never found until, like the Prodigal, we come to ourselves. That is our real coming home. We all suffer from a sense of alienation from who we are: None of us is what we want to be. How many times we are our own worst enemies! When we hurt and need healing love we tend to strike out in anger, pushing healing love farther away. We yearn to be restored to our deepest being, to come home to our true selves, to know that the self we are is deeply and ultimately loved. So we are called to "come home."

JOHN SHELBY SPONG[2]

Then the king will say to those at his right hand, "Come, you that are blessed by my Father, inherit the kingdom prepared for you from the foundation of the world; for I was hungry and you gave me food, I was thirsty and you gave me something to drink, I was a stranger and you welcomed me, I was naked and you gave me clothing, I was sick and you took care of me, I was in prison and you visited me." Then the righteous will answer him, "Lord, when was it that we saw you hungry and gave you food, or thirsty and gave you something to drink? And when was it that we saw you a stranger and welcomed you, or naked and gave you clothing? And when was it that we saw you sick or in prison and visited you?" And the king will answer them, "Truly I tell you, just as you did it to one of the least of these who are members of my family, you did it to me."

MATTHEW 25:34-40

DO THIS IN REMEMBRANCE OF ME!

Introduction

I was confirmed just before my eighth birthday, and I still remember the question I was asked by the bishop: "What did Jesus do at the Last Supper?" I knew the words of the Scripture by heart. I knew them in the Latin language, sacred words pronounced by the priest when all in the church seemed to go silent.

It would be some time before I understood their meaning, and years later before I considered another way of making those words meaningful. I never doubted what I had been taught in elementary and secondary school: that when Jesus said, *Do this in remembrance of me*, he was referring to his death and Resurrection. When the priest takes the bread and cup at Mass and says, *Do this in remembrance of me*, we remember the Last Supper, and the death and Resurrection of our Lord and Savior Jesus Christ.

By the time Saint Paul wrote the first of his letters, around 52 CE, there was already in place the gathering of Christians, the sharing of a meal, the breaking of bread and the blessing of the cup, done in the memory of Jesus the Christ. Wherever Christians gathered, they believed the words of Jesus, "For where two or three are gathered in my name, I am there among them" (Matthew 18:20). Jesus was present in the community, in the readings, and, in a special way, in the breaking of bread and sharing of the cup.

One day I was meditating on this text when I experienced a different thought process. Many questions began to surface as I read and reread the words. It was as if I saw this particular phrase for the first time: *Do this in remembrance of me.*

> *When the hour came, he took his place at the table, and the apostles with him. He said to them, "I have eagerly desired to eat this Passover with you before I suffer; for I tell you, I will not eat it until it is fulfilled in the kingdom of God." Then he took a cup, and after giving thanks he said, "Take this and divide it among yourselves; for I tell you that from now on I will not drink of the fruit of the vine until the kingdom of God comes." Then he took a loaf of bread, and when he had given thanks, he broke it and gave it to them, saying, "This is my body, which is given for you. Do this in remembrance of me." And he did the same with the cup after supper, saying, "This cup that is poured out for you is the new covenant in my blood."*

> LUKE 22:14-20

As I read the words, the thought crossed my mind that Jesus did not say, "Do this in remembrance of *what will happen to me tomorrow.*" He did not say, "After I have risen, the Holy Spirit will remind you that I told you to do this *in memory of my death and resurrection.*" All that to which I had previously given assent-without-question began to unravel. For the first time, the implications of what Jesus really meant when he said, *Do this in remembrance of me*, changed—from words belonging to a fixed ritual, to a series of questions.

What did Jesus *mean* by "do this"? He could not have meant the Passover meal, for it was *already* an annual celebration. What *sense* would it make to just break bread and drink from the cup in remembrance of Jesus? Was there *something more* embedded in the significance of the meal? What was the *relationship* of this meal to all the others Jesus had shared? What are the *implications* of sharing a meal and, in particular, *this* meal?

This was not the first time on my spiritual journey that a meditation on a memorized text suddenly caused me to rethink all I had been told, that I looked at it newly, as if for the first time. Since childhood, I had been told that the Bible was written by human persons through divine inspiration, and as literally as it was said, it was accepted. In other words, the writers of sacred Scripture only wrote what God told them to write. In those days before Vatican Council II, my biblical reading was, for the most part, confined to the four gospels and the Acts of the Apostles.

When I began biblical studies, my literalist mentality was opened like surgery without anesthesia. Almost everything I had been taught, or *thought* I had been taught, was shredded—and I was stumbling to stabilize. I became confused, and somewhat frightened, as my literalist mind came to grips with new insights. I reacted by throwing my *Jerusalem Bible* across the library as I walked out, muttering to myself, "There *is no God*, it's all a pack of lies!"

The stories I'd thought were factual now had new meanings.

Now they were new stories of faith, and my faith was shattering. The Bible as the inspired word of God was changing in context and meaning, and my literalistic mind was suffering from the shock treatment of overload, TMI (too much information). Instead of being fascinated, as I was with philosophy, I was shocked. I reacted. Why should I believe *any* of it? Why should I believe there is a God?

I walked out of the library and into literal and spiritual darkness. Not even a good night's sleep changed my mind. Nothing made sense. And to further confound the situation, I was *still* fascinated by Jesus as a human being.

Jesus intrigued me! At that point in my life most of my weekends were spent working with the poorest of the poor in Dublin, Ireland. These were people sleeping in doorways and in coal sheds, drunks on skid row, attempting sobriety or just existing for the next day's round of cheap alcohol. My heart, soul, and mind were with them—and I had no doubt Jesus was there too. "Just as you did it to one of the least of these who are members of my family, you did it to me" (Matthew 25:40b).

With the help of a compassionate and understanding Scripture professor, I reread the gospels, this time in relation to those parts of the Hebrew Scriptures from which they came. I read about the economic, social, and political life in which Jesus matured before God and his community. I discovered in Jesus a real living human being who loved the God whom he called "Abba."

I'd grown up with injustice, oppression, and domination by a foreign army. Jesus' response to his cultural situation was to reach out. My reaction was entirely different—but that's another story. Now, for the first time in my life, I began to *identify with* Jesus.

Through prayer, meditation, and study I discovered I had *not* stopped believing in God. Rather, I had stopped believing in the God of my childhood: a vengeful, controlling God who kept a ledger of every move I made and every thought that crossed my mind. The God of my childhood was a vindictive, punishing God. Getting into heaven was hard work, requiring extreme vigilance.

As I reformulated my concept of God, I found myself with a loving, caring God, a God who offered me the same choices offered to the people of Israel in the desert.

> *I call heaven and earth to witness against you today*
> *that I have set before you life and death, blessings and*
> *curses. Choose life so that you and your descendants*
> *may live.*
>
> DEUTERONOMY 30:19

I had a *choice.* I was free, not to do as I pleased, but free to do what was pleasing to God: "to do justice, and to love kindness, and to walk humbly with your God" (Micah 6:8b). And I was *chosen.*

> *Before I formed you in the womb I knew you,*
> *and before you were born I consecrated you;*
> *I appointed you a prophet to the nations.*
>
> JEREMIAH 1:5

I was chosen and called by God, to be God's ambassador in this world. An ambassador does not come into the world with his or her own agenda, but represents the mind of the one whom he or she represents. In Jesus, I found the perfect example of God's ambassador. Jesus of Nazareth came to call people back to God—*not* to found a new religion—through an understanding that the "kingdom of God has come near to you" (Luke 10:9b).

Jesus wanted people to experience God as a loving parent. To do that, he practiced what he preached. Then, as now, the people had an ample supply of religious leaders, some of whom were spiritual dictators, or charlatans who harassed them, left them "like sheep without a shepherd" (Mark 6:34b). Consequently, many people found in Jesus a true shepherd. He spoke with authority and lived with integrity. He did not say by *whose* authority he preached or cured, yet one had only to listen to his words to realize that what he preached was the language of the heart—for that *is* the language of religion.

It was the language of the heart that touched the hearts of those who heard him. It was the language of the heart that touched the hearts of those whom he healed. "I know my own and my own know me" (John 10:14b), he said. He was an ambassador, a mirror image of God's love and forgiveness.

Jesus knew the price of being an ambassador. His predecessors, who made the decision to choose life and practice what they preached, were killed, *still* are being killed, but the message lives forever.

> *Jerusalem, Jerusalem, the city that kills the prophets and stones those who are sent to it! How often have I desired to gather your children together as a hen gathers her brood under her wings, and you were not willing!*

> MATTHEW 23:37

To be able to minister in public, knowing that the end result of our work would be death, requires a strength that comes from a power greater than ourselves. To live with integrity demands a life of spirituality connected to a power greater than ourselves, a power of love, trust, and forgiveness that is found personified in the Being we call God. Jesus called this power "Abba," for it was not a stranger to him. He was at one with this power and it with him. "The Father and I are one"(John 10:30), he told us.

How, one might ask, did a boy growing up in an environment in which sick people were outcasts, women were treated as property and widowed women were worse off than most, where children were to be seen and not heard, come to be able to reach out to those who were abandoned by their own society? What was the "difference" in Jesus of Nazareth that made him loved and hated, adored and resented, and in the end, remembered as the greatest influence in the world for two millennia? How did he come to be "the Christ" for his followers? Was it his death? Was it because he had "died to self" long before his public ministry began, and for that reason lived beyond his death? Was it because his life was a living example of daily death to self and a living "Yes" to the will of God? "I seek to do not my own will but the will of him who sent me" (John 5:30b).

To be as a seed in the ground of one's very life is to dissolve in that ground in order to become fruitful. One disappears into Love, in order to "be Love."[3] But this fruitfulness is beyond any planning and any understanding of the person. To be "fruitful" in this sense, one must forget every idea of fruitfulness or productivity, and merely *be.*

After his baptism, Jesus was lead by the Spirit into the

desert. Like all mystics, holy men and women who have that special relationship with God, Jesus withdrew from the world in order to have a time of solitude for deepening his relationship with himself, with God, and with the world to which he would return.

It is well known that those who withdraw from the world in order to commune with God do not run away from the world. Instead, they become more deeply attuned to the pain and suffering and all that is going on in the world than do those who live in its midst on a daily basis.

> Solitude is not withdrawal from ordinary life; solitude is the very ground of ordinary life. It is the very ground of that simple unpretentious, fully human activity by which we quietly earn our daily living and share our experiences with a few intimate friends. But we must learn to know and accept this ground of our being. Only when our activity proceeds out of the ground in which we have consented to be dissolved does it have the divine fruitfulness of love and grace. Only then does it really reach others in true communion.
>
> THOMAS MERTON[4]

What powerful imagery! "Only when our activity proceeds out of the ground in which we have consented to be dissolved." Total freedom! The *choice* to freely and willingly dissolve ourselves, to dissolve into the ground of our being, to ground ourselves into the will of God in order to serve God through serving others, through dying to self. "Unless a grain of wheat falls into the earth and dies, it remains just a single grain" (John 12:24b). The ground on which we stand is holy!

The ground on which we stand *is* holy ground. Each of us, as God's ambassador, is called to change the world in which in we live—whether in our home, our workplace, our parish, or our community. In order for God to use us to reach out to others, we have to die to our selfishness, our petty jealousies, anger, pride, and resentments. We have to die to those things in us that prevent God from using us as a sacred vessel for anointing the sickness of another.

What is offered in this book is an opportunity to reflect on the words, *Do this in remembrance of me,* not just in terms of the Last Supper and Eucharist, but in a way that makes Christ a real presence in every aspect of our lives. Then living becomes a sacred journey; we become sacred vessels of God. In dying to our desires, we are opened to the opportunities to serve God in all people, in the simple tasks of everyday life; and we do them not because "somebody has to do it," but because "just as you did it to one of the least of these who are members of my family, you did it to me"(Matthew 25:40).

To really live, to rise above existence, we are called to do what we do *in remembrance* of the One who taught, by word and example, how to live beyond boundaries. When we live without walls, as truly spiritual people, and do so in everyday simple actions that will make our lives more meaningful, we "will have treasure in heaven" (Luke 18:22c) because we do it *in remembrance* of our Lord and God.

The World in the Time of Jesus

*T*he world into which Jesus came was a psychologically and emotionally unhealthy and violent society. Human rights, as we understand them in today's world, were non-existent. In Israel, Roman brutality and Greek culture intermingled. It was an environment in which some banded together to fight foreign domination and attempt to live in a free Jewish society; others, like Herod and some of the Pharisees, colluded with their cultural enemy for peace at any price; and many more simply went on with life, whether with a sense of enjoyment or in quiet desperation. Galilee, the locale in which Jesus matured, was a community that loved to have a "cause" for which to fight. Its people would fight for almost any cause. Out of this environment came a gentle person who took seriously the core principles of Jewish Law, which he learned in the reading of Scripture.

You shall not take vengeance or bear a grudge against any of your people, but you shall love your neighbor as yourself.

LEVITICUS 19:18a

and

You shall love the LORD your God with all your heart, and with all your soul, and with all your might.

DEUTERONOMY 6:5

Presented with the option of a vindictive God who punishes his enemies or a God of justice and compassion, the young Jesus of Nazareth chose the God who called on his ancestors to "choose life" (Deuteronomy 30:19b). Having experienced the destructive forces of violence from childbirth, he chose an alternative lifestyle. His worldview developed out of his family's values, whose artistic expression kept him in touch with nature and an awareness of the presence of God. Working with difficult types of wood or stone, the young carpenter/stonecutter came to understand what many of his peers failed to learn: how to be patient with difficulties. Perhaps also from his work as a carpenter/stonecutter, he learned the meaning of powerlessness. Wood doesn't always shape the way you want it; stones don't always cut in clean neat corners. In order to get what you want from the wood or the stone, you have to work it with patience, endurance, and love.

Somewhere in his childhood, perhaps in preparation for his Bar Mitzvah, he turned his will and his life over to God. Somewhere, perhaps in the Temple at the age of twelve, he made the decision to choose life and live it to the fullest. He chose to leave with a loving God that which he could not change, and to go on living. To do that, he had to die to self and selfishness; he had to be free to see life for what it is really worth, and to freely decide to be an ambassador of God, a mirror of love and forgiveness. He had to live a life filled with compassion within a secular and religious hostile environment.

Perhaps Jesus developed a strong sense of spiritual security from praying Psalm 37.

> *Do not fret because of the wicked;*
>> *do not be envious of wrongdoers,*
> *for they will soon fade like the grass,*
>> *and wither like the green herb.*
> *Commit your way to the LORD;*
>> *trust in him, and he will act.*
> *He will make your vindication shine like the light,*
>> *and the justice of your cause like the noonday.*
> *Be still before the LORD, and wait patiently for him;*
>> *do not fret over those who prosper in their way,*
>> *over those who carry out evil devices.*
> *For the wicked shall be cut off,*
>> *but those who wait for the LORD shall inherit the land.*
> *….the meek shall inherit the land,*
>> *and delight themselves in abundant prosperity.*

PSALM 37:1-2,5-7,9,11

We can speculate that as this sensitive young Jesus sat on the hillside looking at the vines, he saw in them the image of his homeland, Israel. Perhaps when he was building a winepress he spent some time in a vineyard, and learned that the seed had to die in order to become a vine, that the grapes had to be crushed in order to produce the fruit of the vine. Perhaps when he was building a granary for the wheat, or working for a time in the fields with his uncles or neighbors, he experienced the sowing of the wheat. Some of the seed fell on stony ground, some on limited soil, most of it in good soil—but even there it was not immune to weeds. As a budding mystic and philosopher, Jesus was observant, and thought about how and why things were the way they were.

> The earth is the LORD's and all that is in it,
>   the world, and those who live in it;
> for he has founded it on the seas,
>   and established it on the rivers.

PSALM 24:1-2

Why were bread and the fruit of the vine symbols of life? In order for us to eat and drink those things that give us nourishment, they have to die and be broken. In order for us to love and forgive, we have to die to our selfish and cultural biases. Like Archimedes, running down the street naked, yelling for joy, "Eureka, Eureka!" we can imagine Jesus jumping with excitement in the fields, saying, "I found it. I found it! To live is to die. To live is to die. To die is to live!"

No wonder the rabbis in the Temple were amazed at his wisdom and his questions. Jesus had learned, through prayer and meditation, from observation of life and hands-on experience, what others could not see. And he took it to heart. In the fields, where not even "Solomon in all his glory" (Luke 12:27b) was arrayed like the flowers he picked, Jesus knew he was in his Father's house.

The Implications
of Baptism

As a young adult, I understood baptism to be that time when a person was made a member of the Church; that it was the first sacrament received, and it washed away original sin. In baptism, a person willingly gives himself or herself to God, knowing what is involved in that commitment. Adults who have children and infants baptized take on the responsibility of teaching those little ones the nature of the commitment that was made on their behalf. It is hoped that the child will reaffirm the baptismal commitment in confirmation, and in ritual renewal of baptismal vows throughout life, especially at Easter.

Prayer and meditation, talking and listening to God, bring us to a point where we consciously realize that the *only* power we have is the power to turn our will and our lives over to God. As we consciously come to grips with our essential powerlessness, we also discover the implications of our newfound freedom. Our complete freedom is bounded by our recognition of moral boundaries and responsibility. When we fail, and we *will* fail to some degree, we discover that God is there, within us, and surrounding us with those we need to help heal our brokenness.

In baptism we become members of the community of Christians, and through our baptism we make a covenant with God. Through baptism, we are called to a life of service to God. There are those who are called to be teachers, mechanics, and bankers; doctors, lawyers, and house painters; and any number of other public servants. These vocations are one way in which we utilize the gifts of the Spirit and live out our call to serve. "Here am I; send me!" (Isaiah 6:8b).

After his baptism, Jesus went in search of his vocational identity. He felt the call to be a rabbi, to be a teller of stories that would lift the minds of listeners to God and call them to a deeper relationship with God.

> *But the hour is coming, and is now here, when the true worshipers will worship the Father in spirit and in truth, for the Father seeks such as these to worship him. God is spirit, and those who worship him must worship in spirit and truth.*
>
> JOHN 4:23-24

No longer was Jesus to form tables, chairs, or doorframes, build walls, and set cornerstones. Instead, he was to take down walls and reframe the door through which we were to enter the kingdom. And for those who came to believe in him, he became the cornerstone the builders rejected (see Matthew 21:42; Mark 12:10; Luke 20:17; Acts 4:11).

The question he had to answer was what kind of teacher, what kind of rabbi, would he be? In the desert, as he pondered the meaning of his call to be a rabbi, he was tempted to types of ministry which, while appearing to be for the glory of God, were essentially self-serving and self-gratifying. He was tempted to ministries that were based on emotionalism, sensationalism, and materialism. It was his knowledge of the Scriptures that strengthened Jesus, in each temptation, to take a stand that affirmed for him not only who he was, but also to Whom he belonged.

He was tempted to play on the emotions of those in need, both physically and spiritually. He could meet their needs, but he knew that "one does not live by bread alone" (Luke 4:4b). God's word is full of emotion, but not emotionalism. Was Jesus praying/thinking of Proverbs, or of Psalm 1 or 2?

> *Better is a dry morsel with quiet*
> *than a house full of feasting with strife.*

PROVERBS 17:1

> *Happy are those*
> *who do not follow the advice of the wicked,*
> *or take the path that sinners tread,*
> *or sit in the seat of scoffers;*
> *but their delight is in the law of the LORD,*
> *and on his law they meditate day and night.*

PSALM 1:1-2

> *I will tell of the decree of the LORD:*
> *He said to me, "You are my son;*
> *today I have begotten you.*
> *Happy are all who take refuge in him.*

PSALM 2:7,11d

Jesus was tempted to provide sensational wonders to inspire people. He could make the deaf hear, the blind see, the crippled walk. All of this could bring him fame, even fortune. But he knew better than to "put the Lord your God to the test" (Luke 4:12b). Faith based on sensationalism becomes like the wheat on rocky ground: sudden, shallow, and soon dead. Was he thinking of or praying Psalm 9 or Psalm 40, where one gives thanks to God rather than draw attention to oneself?

> *I will give thanks to the LORD with my whole heart;*
> *I will tell of all your wonderful deeds.*
> *I will be glad and exult in you;*
> *I will sing praise to your name, O Most High.*

PSALM 9:1-2

> *Happy are those who make*
> *the LORD their trust,*
> *who do not turn to the proud,*
> *to those who go astray after false gods.*

PSALM 40:4

What better place to be in, to help the poor, than a position of influence, both politically and financially? There are few financially secure people in positions of power who can withstand the temptations that come with such power. But Jesus understood what was more important: "Worship the Lord your God, and serve only him" (Luke 4:8). Was he thinking of Proverbs?

Riches and honor are with me,
enduring wealth and prosperity.
My fruit is better than gold, even fine gold,
and my yield than choice silver.

PROVERBS 8:18-19

Or was Jesus praying/thinking of Psalm 11 or Psalm 34?

In the LORD I take refuge; how can you say to me,
"Flee like a bird to the mountains;
for look, the wicked bend the bow,
they have fitted their arrow to the string,
to shoot in the dark at the upright in heart.
If the foundations are destroyed,
what can the righteous do?"
For the LORD is righteous;
he loves righteous deeds;
the upright shall behold his face.

PSALM 11:1-3,7

I will bless the LORD at all times;
his praise shall continually be in my mouth.
My soul makes its boast in the LORD;
let the humble hear and be glad.

PSALM 34:1-2

As a human being, Jesus knew the source of his power was a power greater than himself. He called that power "Abba." The ministry of Jesus was to be based on the summation of the commandments.

"You shall love the Lord your God with all your heart, and with all your soul, and with all your mind." This is the greatest and first commandment. And a second is like it: "You shall love your neighbor as yourself."

MATTHEW 22:37-39

The life of Jesus was a life of dying to self, "for I have come down from heaven, not to do my own will, but the will of him who sent me" (John 6:38), a life based on the Scriptures read and psalms prayed.

I say to the LORD, "You are my Lord;
    I have no good apart from you."
I bless the LORD who gives me counsel;
    in the night also my heart instructs me.
I keep the LORD always before me;
    because he is at my right hand,
        I shall not be moved.

PSALM 16:2,7-8

To love ourselves is to come to grips with the basic reality that we are children of God. Even when we do not like the behavior of our brothers and sisters, we cannot judge them; nor can we imitate their negative behavior. We are ambassadors of God, mirrors of God's love, mercy, and forgiveness.

The World of Jesus
of Nazareth

*T*he world into which Jesus was born, and in which he matured, was a sick and violent world. People were mugged and robbed, women were raped, children were to be seen and not heard, and female children were worth their weight in gold only if their fathers could find them a husband. Jesus knew firsthand the "worth" of the life of being human.

Jesus lived in a country dominated by a foreign power that barely tolerated the religious beliefs of his people. It was only natural for many in Galilee to fight this foreign domination they considered a godless enemy. When people are dehumanized, they tend to react with less-than-human behaviors and feel perfectly justified in doing so.

Within Judaism itself, the sect of the Pharisees had, for the most part, become increasingly legalistic. Unfortunately, as in all religions, there were those who believed themselves to be "called" to clarify for others what the laws ought to be for their generation. (It is reported, hopefully jokingly, that after the Second Vatican Council a priest placed a sign outside his church stating, "Come here and you will not only hear the word of God, but *exactly* what he means.") Legalism happens when those in charge become afraid of change, afraid *to* change. Life happens when we choose to live our lives within the boundaries defined by the Law and the Prophets. "You shall love the Lord your God with all your heart, and with all your soul, and with all your strength, and with all your mind; and your neighbor as yourself" (Luke 10:27).

Jesus was born at a time when the straight and narrow between the Law and the Prophets had become the white line in the road. Jesus came, and "in him was life, and the life was the light of all people" (John 1:4). Jesus *chose* life. Life, like good wheat, can grow in the same field as the weeds.

> Only when our activity proceeds out of the ground in which we have consented to be dissolved does it have the divine fruitfulness of love and grace. Only then does it really reach others in true communion.
>
> JOHN DOMINIC CROSSAN[5]

To choose life is to have compassion: to feel *with* and feel *for* those in pain and those in joy. It is to *feel what they feel*, in the very marrow of our bones, without losing ourselves in the process. To choose life is to acknowledge the reality of a pain-filled world and be able to offer hope and consolation. It is to offer a lasting inner peace in the midst of a storm; to *be a part of* and yet *not belong to* the sickness. To choose life is to be *consciously aware of the presence of God* in time and space, in sacred localities and in all localities, in particular people and in all people. To choose life is to be conscious of the clear sky and the hurricane, the free and the imprisoned, the sick and the healthy, without letting the contradictions change our perception of what is true.

The life of Jesus was a life based on being God's ambassador. Jesus touched the lepers—both physically and emotionally—and in touching them he made them whole. Perhaps he had discovered, from his days of meditation, that what the Scriptures say is true: "A tranquil mind gives life to the flesh" (Proverbs 14:30a).

Children came to Jesus and were not afraid of him. He picked them up and made them feel important, and he taught about the kingdom of God through them.

Truly I tell you, unless you change and become like children, you will never enter the kingdom of heaven. Let the little children come to me, and do not stop them; for it is to such as these that the kingdom of heaven belongs.

MATTHEW 18:3; 19:14

To get into the kingdom of God, we are to become like little children: to be a people who have not lost our sense of awe and wonder about the sun, moon, and stars, the rainbow, and the flowers in the fields; to be a people who know they depend upon a loving mother or father to care for them, and who place their wholehearted trust in that parent. To get into the kingdom of God, we have to become a people who have not as yet learned how to hate and to judge others. "Do not judge, and you will not be judged" (Luke 6:37a). Was Jesus thinking of the biblical proverbs?

Even children make themselves known by their acts,
by whether what they do is pure and right.

PROVERBS 20:11

And now, my children, listen to me:
happy are those who keep my ways.
Hear instruction and be wise,
and do not neglect it.
Happy is the one who listens to me,
watching daily at my gates,
waiting beside my doors.
For whoever finds me finds life
and obtains favor from the LORD;
but those who miss me injure themselves;
all who hate me love death.

PROVERBS 8:32-36

Women came to him. Women were an integral part of his inner circle of close intimate friends.

Soon afterwards he went on through cities and villages, proclaiming and bringing the good news of the kingdom of God. The twelve were with him, as well as some women who had been cured of evil spirits and infirmities: Mary, called Magdalene, from whom seven demons had gone out, and Joanna, the wife of Herod's steward Chuza, and Susanna, and many others, who provided for them out of their resources.

LUKE 8:1-3

Jesus was from the lineage of David, and there were women in that line whose character may have been questionable, but they were strong women and women of faith. Jesus knew that what Proverbs said of a wife was true of many women.

A capable wife who can find?
She is far more precious than jewels.
The heart of her husband trusts in her,
and he will have no lack of gain.
She does him good, and not harm,
all the days of her life.
Strength and dignity are her clothing,
and she laughs at the time to come.
She opens her mouth with wisdom,
and the teaching of kindness is on her tongue.
She looks well to the ways of her household,
and does not eat the bread of idleness.
Her children rise up and call her happy;
her husband too, and he praises her:

PROVERBS 31:10-12,25-28

The blind, the deaf, the mentally and physically ill—all found him—and in him they found life and received life because life flowed out from him.

And wherever he went, into villages or cities or farms,
they laid the sick in the marketplaces, and begged him
that they might touch even the fringe of his cloak; and
all who touched it were healed.

MARK 6:56

The people found compassion and forgiveness. Only those who are comfortable with themselves, who recognize in another human being the same source of their own life and see the potential for greater things that is inherent within, can give life through love and forgiveness. To forgive is to elevate the "fallen one" to a status equal to our own, to stand with that person, and ultimately to tell others—whether together or after having continued on our separate ways—of the great things God has done for us.

To the Israelites, the Romans were enemies who held the land by brute force. The *Pax Romana*, the peace of Rome, was bought through intimidation and making an art of crucifixion. Yet, for Jesus, the Romans were not his personal enemies. Was it because he believed what Proverbs says?

> *Do not rejoice when your enemies fall,*
> > *and do not let your heart be glad when they stumble,*
> *or else the LORD will see it and be displeased,*
> > *and turn away his anger from them.*
> *If your enemies are hungry, give them bread to eat;*
> > *and if they are thirsty, give them water to drink;*
> *for you will heap coals of fire on their heads,*
> > *and the LORD will reward you.*

PROVERBS 24:17-18; 25:21-22

Perhaps the Romans recognized in Jesus a holy man who was not legalistic, who saw the world through a different lens. Perhaps they recognized in Jesus a power not found in their own priests, nor in the religious establishment of Israel at the time. Perhaps they recognized the power of love and reconciliation, and its impact on one's health. Whatever it was, they recognized something in Jesus; they asked him to cure their servants and their children.

We cannot help but conclude that, because Jesus taught by word and example, he was telling us to touch people—mentally, emotionally, physically, and spiritually. Can we also conclude that when he said *Do this in remembrance of me* he was thinking of all those he touched and made whole, of those who came to him broken, desperate, and hurt? Perhaps he was inspired by the words of the Lord to Isaiah.

> *For I am about to create new heavens*
> *and a new earth;*
> *the former things shall not be remembered*
> *or come to mind.*
> *But be glad and rejoice forever*
> *in what I am creating;*
> *for I am about to create Jerusalem as a joy,*
> *and its people as a delight.*
> *I will rejoice in Jerusalem,*
> *and delight in my people;*
> *no more shall the sound of weeping be heard in it,*
> *or the cry of distress.*

ISAIAH 65:17-19

Perhaps Jesus was conscious the Spirit of God being with him, to set free those who were captive to illness, those imprisoned in their emotional/psychological prisons.

The spirit of the Lord GOD is upon me,
    because the LORD has anointed me;
he has sent me to bring good news to the oppressed,
    to bind up the brokenhearted,
to proclaim liberty to the captives,
    and release to the prisoners;
to proclaim the year of the LORD's favor,
    and the day of vengeance of our God;
    to comfort all who mourn;
to provide for those who mourn in Zion—
    to give them a garland instead of ashes,
the oil of gladness instead of mourning,
    the mantle of praise instead of a faint spirit.

ISAIAH 61:1-3b

Jesus was conscious of the Spirit of God being with him as he shared the Good News with those who did not count in society. His memory was formed in the Scriptures he read, through which he came to know a God of love and compassion. Jesus wanted people to remember, to put together, to integrate their body, soul, mind, and become free to be ambassadors for God.

We are called *not* to follow Jesus, but to *imitate* him. If we take this seriously, then we might ask in a simplistic manner, What Would Jesus Do? The answer, if we are serious, evolves into a more difficult question, one that perhaps Jesus would ask: What Would Justice Demand?[6]

It is the answer to this last question that makes us think from a new and deeper perspective, and respond with compassion to Jesus' command: **Do this in remembrance of me** (Luke 22:19b).

Love Your Neighbor

*J*ust then a lawyer stood up to test Jesus. "Teacher," he said, "what must I do to inherit eternal life?" He said to him, "What is written in the law? What do you read there?" He answered, "You shall love the Lord your God with all your heart, and with all your soul, and with all your strength, and with all your mind; and your neighbor as yourself." And he said to him, "You have given the right answer; do this, and you will live."

But wanting to justify himself, he asked Jesus, "And who is my neighbor?" Jesus replied, "A man was going down from Jerusalem to Jericho, and fell into the hands of robbers, who stripped him, beat him, and went away, leaving him half dead. Now by chance a priest was going down that road; and when he saw him, he passed by on the other side. So likewise a Levite, when he came to the place and saw him, passed by on the other side. But a Samaritan while traveling came near him; and when he saw him, he was moved with pity. He went to him and bandaged his wounds, having poured oil and *wine on them. Then he put him on his own animal, brought him to an inn, and took care of him. The next day he took out two denarii, gave them to the innkeeper, and said, 'Take care of him; and when I come back, I will repay you whatever more you spend.' Which of these three, do you think, was a neighbor to the man who fell into the hands of the robbers?" He said, "The one who showed him mercy." Jesus said to him, "Go and do likewise."*

LUKE 10:25-37

Consider…

- ✎ When was the last time it really cost me—in terms of time, personal energy, and resources—to care for another human being?
- ✎ What are the justice issues in this story for my community today?
- ✎ What are some justice issues from this story for the Church today?
- ✎ What Would Justice Demand in this story today?
- ✎ How does dehumanizing another human effect my relationship to myself, others, and God?
- ✎ How have I—in what I have said or failed to say, done or failed to do—contributed to negativity in my workplace, community, Church?
- ✎ How did this Samaritan die to self in order to help this stranger?

Remember…

Those who oppress the poor insult their Maker.

PROVERBS 14:31a

You shall not defraud your neighbor; you shall not steal.

LEVITICUS 19:13a-b

You shall not take vengeance or bear a grudge against any of your people, but you shall love your neighbor as yourself: I am the LORD.

LEVITICUS 19:18

Jesus said, *Go and do likewise.*

LUKE 10:37b

DO THIS IN REMEMBRANCE OF ME.

Pray…

Lord Jesus Christ, I ask forgiveness for the narrow-minded bigotry, classism, parochialism, racism, etc. that prevent me from seeing all people as my sisters and brothers. Help me, Lord. Send your Holy Spirit to enlighten me, that I may see the world as you see it, and give me the courage to work for justice and peace in the community in which I live, that I may set the example of loving others by treating everyone with respect and dignity. Help me to see that in breaking bread and drinking from the same cup, I make your presence real in the world around me only insofar as I treat others as I would like to be treated… and do it in remembrance of you. Amen

Forgive One Another

*T*hen Peter came and said to him, "Lord, if another member of the church sins against me, how often should I forgive? As many as seven times?" Jesus said to him, "Not seven times, but, I tell you, seventy-seven times.

"For this reason the kingdom of heaven may be compared to a king who wished to settle accounts with his slaves. When he began the reckoning, one who owed him ten thousand talents was brought to him; and, as he could not pay, his lord ordered him to be sold, together with his wife and children and all his possessions, and payment to be made. So the slave fell on his knees before him, saying, 'Have patience with me, and I will pay you everything.' And out of pity for him, the lord of that slave released him and forgave him the debt. But that same slave, as he went out, came upon one of his fellow slaves who owed him a hundred denarii; and seizing him by the throat, he said, 'Pay what you owe.' Then his fellow slave fell down and pleaded with him, 'Have patience with me, and I will pay you.' But he* *refused; then he went and threw him into prison until he would pay the debt. When his fellow slaves saw what had happened, they were greatly distressed, and they went and reported to their lord all that had taken place. Then his lord summoned him and said to him, 'You wicked slave! I forgave you all that debt because you pleaded with me. Should you not have had mercy on your fellow slave, as I had mercy on you?' And in anger his lord handed him over to be tortured until he would pay his entire debt. So my heavenly Father will also do to every one of you, if you do not forgive your brother or sister from your heart."*

MATTHEW 18:21-35

Consider…

- ✧ Describe how you would feel if your debts were eliminated.
- ✧ How many times in the past month have you asked God for forgiveness?
- ✧ List five people to whom you need to go and say, "I forgive you."

1. _____
2. _____
3. _____
4. _____
5. _____

- ∽ How has keeping grudges and resentments affected you emotionally, physically, psychologically, and spiritually? What would it take for you to let go of them?
- ∽ How did the slave owner die to self in order to forgive such a debt?
- ∽ What prevented the slave who had been forgiven from dying to self to help a fellow slave?
- ∽ What Would Justice Demand of me today in my relationships with my family? friends? neighbors? community?

Remember...

"Say to Joseph: I beg you, forgive the crime of your brothers and the wrong they did in harming you." Now therefore please forgive the crime of the servants of the God of your father.

GENESIS 50:17

No longer shall they teach one another, or say to each other, "Know the LORD," for they shall all know me, from the least of them to the greatest, says the LORD; for I will forgive their iniquity, and remember their sin no more.

JEREMIAH 31:34

For your name's sake, O LORD,
pardon my guilt, for it is great.

PSALM 25:11

Do not withhold good from those to whom it is due,
when it is in your power to do it.

PROVERBS 3:27

Jesus said, ***In everything do to others***
as you would have them do to you.

MATTHEW 7:12a

DO THIS IN REMEMBRANCE OF ME.

Pray…

Forgive me, Father, for I have sinned. I have held grudges, participated in gossip about a neighbor, caused a coworker to lose his job because I believed it was right to tell the truth about his addictive behavior. I ask forgiveness for my silence, and for the lack of courage to reach out to those whom I could have assisted. I ask forgiveness for choosing social status that sets boundaries around where and with whom I could "be Christian." Fill my heart with love, that I may let go of my anger. Increase my trust in you, and liberate me from my selfish prison so that I may do your will. Help me, Lord, to see that in breaking bread and drinking from the same cup, I make your presence real in the world around me only insofar as I forgive and ask for forgiveness…and do it in remembrance of you. Amen

The Prodigal Son and the Forgiving Father

*T*hen Jesus said, "There was a man who had two sons. The younger of them said to his father, 'Father, give me the share of the property that will belong to me.' So he divided his property between them. A few days later the younger son gathered all he had and traveled to a distant country, and there he squandered his property in dissolute living. When he had spent everything, a severe famine took place throughout that country, and he began to be in need. So he went and hired himself out to one of the citizens of that country, who sent him to his fields to feed the pigs. He would gladly have filled himself with the pods that the pigs were eating; and no one gave him anything. But when he came to himself he said, 'How many of my father's hired hands have bread enough and to spare, but here I am dying of hunger! I will get up and go to my father, and I will say to him, "Father, I have sinned against heaven and before you; I am no longer worthy to be called your son; treat me like one of your hired hands."' So he set off *and went to his father. But while he was still far off, his father saw him and was filled with compassion; he ran and put his arms around him and kissed him. Then the son said to him, 'Father, I have sinned against heaven and before you; I am no longer worthy to be called your son.' But the father said to his slaves, 'Quickly, bring out a robe—the best one—and put it on him; put a ring on his finger and sandals on his feet. And get the fatted calf and kill it, and let us eat and celebrate; for this son of mine was dead and is alive again; he was lost and is found!' And they began to celebrate.*

"Now his elder son was in the field; and when he came and approached the house, he heard music and dancing. He called one of the slaves and asked what was going on. He replied, 'Your brother has come, and your father has killed the fatted calf, because he has got him back safe and sound.' Then he became angry and refused to go in. His father came out and began to plead with him. But he answered his father, 'Listen! For all these years I have been working like a slave for you, and I have never disobeyed your command; yet you have never given me even a young goat so that I might celebrate with my friends. But when this son of yours came back, who has devoured your property with prostitutes, you killed the fatted calf for him!' Then the father said to him, 'Son, you are always with me, and all that is mine is yours. But we had to celebrate and rejoice, because this brother of yours was dead and has come to life; he was lost and has been found.'"

LUKE 15:11-32

Consider...

- As a prodigal son/daughter in need of forgiveness, I feel_____.
- Sometimes I am more like the older brother: jealous, can't wish another person good fortune. I can't welcome home those who are willing to take the risks I am unable or unwilling to take, because I need to "play it safe," and I feel

  _____.
- The most difficult thing about forgiveness, for me, is_____.
- How did this father die to self to be on the lookout for his son?
- How did the prodigal son die to self in order to return home?
- What attitudes did the older brother have that prevented him from dying-to-self to welcome home his wayward brother?
- What Would Justice Demand of me today?

Remember...

Indeed the LORD will vindicate his people,
have compassion on his servants,
when he sees that their power is gone,
neither bond nor free remaining.

DEUTERONOMY 32:36

But you are a God ready to forgive, gracious and merciful, slow to anger and abounding in steadfast love, and you did not forsake them.

Jesus said, *Do not judge, and you will not be judged.*

LUKE 6:37a

DO THIS IN REMEMBRANCE OF ME.

Pray...

Heavenly Father, I have judged others mentally, verbally, and in my body language. I have judged my brothers and sisters for their lack of vocabulary and fine clothing, by their occupation and lack of occupation. I have judged them by their actions and reactions, or response to the world around them. Now, O Lord, I hang my head in shame. Lord, I look in the mirror and see I too am your child. I look in the mirror and see that we are all the same regardless of our vocabulary, occupation, or lifestyle.

Thank you, Lord, for opening my eyes. Help me to be like Zacchaeus by being generous in my amends, and to see that, in breaking bread and drinking from the same cup, I can make your presence real in the world around me only through service to others, and do it in remembrance of you. Amen

A Sense of Compassion

When he saw the crowds, he had compassion for them, because they were harassed and helpless, like sheep without a shepherd.

MATTHEW 9:36

When he went ashore, he saw a great crowd; and he had compassion for them and cured their sick.

MATTHEW 14:14

Then Jesus called his disciples to him and said, "I have compassion for the crowd, because they have been with me now for three days and have nothing to eat; and I do not want to send them away hungry, for they might faint on the way."

MATTHEW 15:32

Moved with compassion, Jesus touched their eyes. Immediately they regained their sight and followed him.

MATTHEW 20:34

Moved with pity, Jesus stretched out his hand and touched him, and said to him, "I do choose. Be made clean!"

Consider...

- ᐳ How consciously aware are you of the level of poverty *in your community* (not just that of the working poor who work two to three jobs to make ends meet)?
- ᐳ How does feeling hungry affect you psychologically, emotionally, and socially?
- ᐳ How have you contributed to the alleviation of poverty in your community?
- ᐳ How are you connected to those resources in your community that serve the poorest of the poor?
- ᐳ List five ways you are affected by the knowledge that in your community there are people who are not just poor but are, in fact, living in poverty?

1. _____
2. _____
3. _____
4. _____
5. _____

- ᐳ **What Would Justice Demand** of you, your church, and your community today?

Remember…

The LORD would be moved to pity by their groaning because of those who persecuted and oppressed them.

JUDGES 2:18b

When they turned and cried to you, you heard from heaven, and many times you rescued them according to your mercies.

NEHEMIAH 9:28b

Gracious is the LORD, and righteous;
*   our God is merciful.*

PSALM 116:5

The rich and the poor have this in common:
*   the LORD is the maker of them all.*

PROVERBS 22:2

Stretch out your hand to the poor,
*   so that your blessing may be complete.*

SIRACH 7:32

Jesus said, *I was hungry and you gave me food.*

MATTHEW 25:35a

DO THIS IN REMEMBRANCE OF ME.

Pray…

Heavenly Father, there are times when I feel overwhelmed by the physical, emotional, intellectual, and spiritual poverty in this world. There are times when I want to do something but do not know where to start, and then I procrastinate in the hope that someone else will do it. Lord, I feel for others, but I do not always have compassion. Send your Holy Spirit, Lord, to open my eyes to see your goodness in every human being. Fill my heart with true compassion, that I may do all I can in the world around me to make those with whom I come in contact, and those I know about but do not always see, feel a sense of worth and dignity. Help me, Lord, to see that in breaking bread and drinking from the same cup, I make your presence real in the world around me only insofar as I become a compassionate co-creator of this world, not just a church-going bystander, and do it in remembrance of you. Amen

The Lost Sheep

*W*hat do you think? If a shepherd has a hundred sheep, and one of them has gone astray, does he not leave the ninety-nine on the mountains and go in search of the one that went astray? And if he finds it, truly I tell you, he rejoices over it more than over the ninety-nine that never went astray.

MATTHEW 18:12-13

Which one of you, having a hundred sheep and losing one of them, does not leave the ninety-nine in the wilderness and go after the one that is lost until he finds it? When he has found it, he lays it on his shoulders and rejoices. And when he comes home, he calls together his friends and neighbors, saying to them, "Rejoice with me, for I have found my sheep that was lost."

LUKE 15:4-6

The hired hand, who is not the shepherd and does not own the sheep, sees the wolf coming and leaves the sheep and runs away—and the wolf snatches them and scatters

them. The hired hand runs away because a hired hand
does not care for the sheep. I am the good shepherd. I
know my own and my own know me.

JOHN 10:12-14

Abuse in families is a sad part of human history that continues to repeat itself. The following short scenario is a case in point.

"Mrs. Caldwell, it is none of my business, but I want you to know I care about your son. You may not choose to believe me, but you need to know your son is selling drugs." The sweat was rolling down John's back as the words came out. He was well aware that his neighbor, an intelligent woman, who through a sad and sudden situation had become a single parent and widow, loved her son and believed him wholeheartedly. He was an only child, fifteen years of age, and for the past four years "the man of the house."

It was another two years before Mrs. Caldwell, a victim of her son's physical abuse, came to grips with the painful reality that her son was walking in the footsteps of his father's youthful days. She did not want to believe it.

Consider…

- ✎ Who among my family, friends, church or work acquaintances has gone astray by gambling, drugs, alcohol, and/or unhealthy relationships? Five things I have said negatively about them are:

1. _____
2. _____
3. _____
4. _____
5. _____

↬ What have I done to intervene or offer assistance?

↬ What are the risks involved in seeking after the one who is lost?

↬ What would have happened if Jesus said, "I am not my brother's keeper"?

↬ Twelve Step Programs welcome back, with joy and ritual and without question, those who have relapsed and want to begin again. What can we, as Church, learn from AA?

↬ How did members of Twelve Step Programs learn to die to self in order to welcome others back?

↬ What has happened to us, the people of God, that we have such difficulty dying to self and really welcoming back to the Lord's Table those who have cut themselves off from God?

Remember…

Glory in his holy name;
let the hearts of those who seek the LORD rejoice.

1 CHRONICLES 16:10

I will exult and rejoice in your steadfast love,
because you have seen my affliction;

PSALM 31:7a

Jesus said, ***Today salvation has come to this house,***
because he too is a son of Abraham.
For the Son of Man came to seek out and to save the lost.

LUKE 19:9-10

DO THIS IN REMEMBRANCE OF ME.

Pray…

Lord Jesus Christ, I do not want to be my brother's keeper. This world is dangerous, and it's not safe anymore to become involved in the lives of others. I believe this, and yet I know that this world is much safer than the world in which you matured before God and your community. You overcame prejudice and fear of community rejection in order to touch the lepers, the blind, the sick. No one, Lord, was beyond your reach. Help me to overcome my fear of becoming involved with my sisters and brothers in need. Help me, Lord, to see that in breaking bread and drinking from the same cup, I make your presence real in the world around me only insofar as I become my brother's keeper, and do it in remembrance of you. Amen

Love Your Enemies

*B*ut I say to you that listen, Love your enemies, do good to those who hate you, bless
those who curse you, pray for those who
abuse you. If anyone strikes you on the cheek, offer the
other also; and from anyone who takes away your coat
do not withhold even your shirt. Give to everyone who
begs from you; and if anyone takes away your goods,
do not ask for them again. But love your enemies, do
good, and lend, expecting nothing in return. Your reward will be great, and you will be children of the Most
High; for he is kind to the ungrateful and the wicked.
Be merciful, just as your Father is merciful.*

LUKE 6:27-30,35-36

*In everything do to others as you would have them do
to you; for this is the law and the prophets.*

MATTHEW 7:12

A young man sat in the back of a transport truck with six British soldiers. They were part of a convoy helping him transport handicapped children across Northern Ireland at the height of the troubles in the early 1970's. Since childhood, although he had never met anyone from England, he had learned to hate the British and everything about them. The soldiers were about his own age or slightly younger. Realizing he had approximately a three hour trip ahead of him with this "enemy" who was doing him a favor, he decided to try and have polite conversation. He learned they had been stationed in Germany, and the last part of their tour of duty was to serve in Northern Ireland. To his surprise, he discovered none of them had wanted to come here. He also learned they did not like doing home searches, as one of them told him, "I have three sisters. I would not like anyone going into their room and searching through their wardrobes." Another soldier spoke up and told him how his best friend of seventeen years had been killed beside him the previous day. This young British soldier, sitting there with a machine gun, began to cry. The young man looked at his enemy and realized: "These are not my enemy. I am the enemy, I am my own enemy."

Consider…

- ✏ How has prejudice affected your life?
- ✏ How has prejudice affected the way you treat those who are different from you?
- ✏ What difference—emotionally, psychologically, physically, and spiritually—does it make to you to bless the person who curses you?

- What justice issues are involved in loving one's enemies, doing good to those who curse us?
- By dying to self, what do we learn by making contact with our "enemy" or those against whom we are prejudiced?
- By dying to self, how can God use us in our relationships with those with whom we do not want to communicate?
- How have you emotionally imprisoned yourself through prejudice and hatred?

Remember…

You shall not hate in your heart anyone of your kin; you shall reprove your neighbor, or you will incur guilt yourself. You shall not take vengeance or bear a grudge against any of your people, but you shall love your neighbor as yourself: I am the LORD.

LEVITICUS 19:17-18

If your enemies are hungry, give them bread to eat;
    and if they are thirsty, give them water to drink;
for you will heap coals of fire on their heads,
    and the LORD will reward you.

PROVERBS 25:21-22

Jesus said, *Love your enemies.*

LUKE 6:35a

DO THIS IN REMEMBRANCE OF ME.

Pray...

Heavenly Father, in church we learn to love our enemies, but in the real world this is not an accepted value. We dehumanize our enemies so that we can mock them, spit on them, beat them, and even kill them.

Lord Jesus Christ, you too were taught to hate the Romans, not to speak to Samaritans, not to touch the lepers. Yet, Lord, you loved the Romans, cured their children and slaves, you spat on the ground and helped the blind to see. Help me to understand that in breaking bread and drinking from the same cup, I make your presence real in the world around me only insofar as I practice the power of true and unconditional love, and do it in remembrance of you. Amen

Give Me to Drink

*N*ow *when Jesus learned that the Pharisees
had heard, "Jesus is making and baptiz-
ing more disciples than John" —although
it was not Jesus himself but his disciples who baptized—
he left Judea and started back to Galilee. But he had to go
through Samaria. So he came to a Samaritan city called
Sychar, near the plot of ground that Jacob had given to
his son Joseph. Jacob's well was there, and Jesus, tired out
by his journey, was sitting by the well. It was about noon.*

*A Samaritan woman came to draw water, and Jesus
said to her, "Give me a drink." (His disciples had gone
to the city to buy food.) The Samaritan woman said to
him, "How is it that you, a Jew, ask a drink of me, a
woman of Samaria?" (Jews do not share things in common with Samaritans.) Jesus answered her, "If you
knew the gift of God, and who it is that is saying to
you, 'Give me a drink,' you would have asked him, and
he would have given you living water." The woman
said to him, "Sir, you have no bucket, and the well is
deep. Where do you get that living water? Are you*

greater than our ancestor Jacob, who gave us the well, and with his sons and his flocks drank from it?" Jesus said to her, "Everyone who drinks of this water will be thirsty again, but those who drink of the water that I will give them will never be thirsty. The water that I will give will become in them a spring of water gushing up to eternal life." The woman said to him, "Sir, give me this water, so that I may never be thirsty or have to keep coming here to draw water."

Jesus said to her, "Go, call your husband, and come back." The woman answered him, "I have no husband." Jesus said to her, "You are right in saying, 'I have no husband'; for you have had five husbands, and the one you have now is not your husband. What you have said is true!" The woman said to him, "Sir, I see that you are a prophet. Our ancestors worshiped on this mountain, but you say that the place where people must worship is in Jerusalem." Jesus said to her, "Woman, believe me, the hour is coming when you will worship the Father neither on this mountain nor in Jerusalem. You worship what you do not know; we worship what we know, for salvation is from the Jews. But the hour is coming, and is now here, when the true worshipers will worship the Father in spirit and truth, for the Father seeks such as these to worship him. God is spirit, and those who worship him must worship in spirit and truth." The woman said to him, "I know that Messiah is coming" (who is called Christ). "When he comes, he will proclaim all things to us." Jesus said to her, "I am he, the one who is speaking to you."

Just then his disciples came. They were astonished that he was speaking with a woman, but no one said, "What do you want?" or, "Why are you speaking with her?" Then the woman left her water jar and went back to the city. She said to the people, "Come and see a man who told me everything I have ever done! He cannot be the Messiah, can he?" They left the city and were on their way to him.

Meanwhile the disciples were urging him, "Rabbi, eat something." But he said to them, "I have food to eat that you do not know about." So the disciples said to one another, "Surely no one has brought him something to eat?" Jesus said to them, "My food is to do the will of him who sent me and to complete his work. Do you not say, 'Four months more, then comes the harvest'? But I tell you, look around you, and see how the fields are ripe for harvesting. The reaper is already receiving wages and is gathering fruit for eternal life, so that sower and reaper may rejoice together. For here the saying holds true, 'One sows and another reaps.' I sent you to reap that for which you did not labor. Others have labored, and you have entered into their labor."

Many Samaritans from that city believed in him because of the woman's testimony, "He told me everything I have ever done."

JOHN 4:1-39

Consider...

- What are the justice issues in this story?
- How did this woman die to self to talk to Jesus, a Jew?
- How did Jesus of Nazareth, the Galilean, die to self to talk to a woman from Sychar?
- What would it take for you to die to self to have this wellspring of water?
- Do you crave that wellspring of water enough to die to self?
- What Would Justice Demand of you today in relation to those who have no voice? those who have no rights? those who have no one or nothing?

Remember...

Then he said to her, "Please give me a little water to drink; for I am thirsty." So she opened a skin of milk and gave him a drink and covered him.

JUDGES 4:19

Give instruction to the wise,
*   and they will become wiser still;*
*   teach the righteous and they will gain in learning.*
The fear of the LORD is the beginning of wisdom,
*   and the knowledge of the Holy One is insight.*

PROVERBS 9:9-10

My soul thirsts for God, for the living God.

PSALM 42:2a

Jesus said, *I was thirsty and*
you gave me something to drink.

MATTHEW 25:35b

DO THIS IN REMEMBRANCE OF ME.

Pray…

Lord God, I never thought I thirsted for anything. I
have never known physical thirst, nor have I, until
now, thirsted for anything. As I reread this story, I
find myself dry in the throat as I experience a sense
of guilt for not speaking out for those with no voice.
I am dry in the throat because I know my silence has
left me devoid of words, and my superficial relationship to you leaves me thirsting now for the grace you
have already offered me. Help me, Lord, to understand that in breaking bread and drinking from the
same cup, I make your presence real in the world
around me only insofar as I speak to and for the
voiceless, speak to and for those who are
marginalized, make their presence and their worth
known, and do it in remembrance of you. Amen

The Gift
of Friendship

*S*ix days before the Passover Jesus came to
Bethany, the home of Lazarus, whom he
had raised from the dead. There they gave a
dinner for him. Martha served, and Lazarus was one
of those at the table with him. Mary took a pound of
costly perfume made of pure nard, anointed Jesus' feet,
and wiped them with her hair.

JOHN 12:1-3a

*Just then some men came, carrying a paralyzed man
on a bed. They were trying to bring him in and lay
him before Jesus; but finding no way to bring him in
because of the crowd, they went up on the roof and let
him down with his bed through the tiles into the middle
of the crowd in front of Jesus. When he saw their faith,
he said, "Friend, your sins are forgiven you."*

LUKE 5:18-20

Consider...

- ✦ Mary was sensitive to the unspoken pain of Jesus and he permitted her to anoint him as one would anoint the sick. What does this say about Mary? about Jesus?
- ✦ When was the last time you were sensitive to the unspoken physical/emotional pain of another?
- ✦ How do you give permission for others to care for you?
- ✦ How does it make you feel when someone is sensitive to your unspoken pain?
- ✦ List three people who have reached out to you in the past six months.

    1. _____
    2. _____
    3. _____

- ✦ Consciously pray for them daily for the next week.
- ✦ What Would Justice Demand in caring for another human being?

Remember...

Do not forsake your friend or the friend of your parent.
PROVERBS 27:10a

Faithful friends are beyond price;
    no amount can balance their worth.
Faithful friends are life-saving medicine;
    and those who fear the Lord will find them.

Those who fear the Lord direct their friendship aright,
for as they are, so are their neighbors also.

SIRACH 6:15-17

Some friends play at friendship
but a true friend sticks closer than one's nearest kin.

PROVERBS 18:24

Jesus said, *Do this, as often as you drink it,*
in remembrance of me.

1 CORINTHIANS 11:25b

DO THIS IN REMEMBRANCE OF ME.

Pray...

Heavenly Father, we like to differentiate between friends and acquaintances. This seems to make it easier to judge who to trust and who to "watch out for." God, it is so easy to judge, divide, and separate our sisters and brothers into groups labeled for special occasions and gifts given.

Lord Jesus Christ, send your Holy Spirit to open my eyes and heart, to see all my sisters and brothers as friends in need of love, forgiveness, mercy, and compassion. Help me, Lord, to understand that in breaking bread and drinking from the same cup, I make your presence real in the world around me only insofar as I become a friend to those whom I have treated as strangers and acquaintances, and do it in remembrance of you. Amen

The Healing
Power of Touch

A leper came to him begging him, and kneeling he said to him, "If you choose, you can make me clean." Moved with pity, Jesus stretched out his hand and touched him, and said to him, "I do choose. Be made clean!"

MARK 1:40-41

Then Jesus laid his hands on his eyes again; and he looked intently and his sight was restored, and he saw everything clearly.

MARK 8:25

When Jesus entered Peter's house, he saw his mother-in-law lying in bed with a fever; he touched her hand, and the fever left her.

MATTHEW 8:14-15a

It is said that people can walk briskly through the packed streets of New York without touching each other or making eye contact. We walk so fast we create our own glass wall. Such is our society today. In large cities and small towns, people are afraid to get involved. Two people can be sitting next to each other and be worlds apart. We are afraid to touch one another, and in our fear we do not realize our God-given potential to heal.

There is a story told of a man who was admitted to a hospital in a coma. He had no identification on him. For eight weeks, a nurse ended her shift by patting his foot and saying to him, "See you tomorrow, Jack." One evening, as she completed her ritual and was about to close the door, a voice said, "My name is John." He recounted later that he could feel her hand on his foot each evening, although he could not open his eyes or speak.

To touch another human being is to let that person know you care. More often than not, nothing need be said. A warm hug, a handshake, eye contact, all have the power to let someone know you are very present to him, that you care for and about her.

To touch is to make oneself really present to someone who is hurting. We can be a conduit for the blessing and the healing power of God to that person, regardless of his or her religious belief. We can be a stabilizing force in an otherwise chaotic and pain-filled world, even should the person say, "I'm okay."

We touch people intellectually when we engage them in conversation, when we draw out from them their beliefs, their hopes, their dreams, and their thoughts.

We touch people emotionally when we share with them

who we are at that given point in time; when we identify with their emotions; when we communicate at a level where we can feel their pain and their joy.

We touch people physically (appropriately, and with their permission) to anoint, to hold, to congratulate, to caress, to say farewell or welcome back; and in all instances to share with them, through the gift of touch, a sense of our real presence to them and theirs to us.

We touch people socially when we weave together the various strands of the social fabric of community life so that the silk and the sackcloth, the leather and the vinyl are so interwoven as to be experienced as interconnected fabrics, holding together the framework of community.

Reflecting on the Rembrandt painting of the Prodigal Son, author Henri Nouwen writes about the hands of the father.

In them mercy becomes flesh; upon them forgiveness, reconciliation, and healing come together, and through them, not only the tired son, but also the worn-out father find their rest. From the moment I first saw [the painting] I felt drawn to those hands. I did not fully understand why. But gradually over the years I have come to know those hands. They have held me from the hour of my conception, they welcomed me at my birth, held me close to my mother's breast, fed me, and kept me warm. They have protected me in times of danger and consoled me in times of grief. They have waved me good-bye and always welcomed me back. Those hands are God's hands. They are also the hands of my parents, teachers, friends, healers, and all those whom God has given me to remind me how safely I am held.[7]

Consider…

- ⤍ Who are the untouchables in your community, that need you to reach out and touch them?
- ⤍ What difference did it make to you to reach out and touch someone?
- ⤍ Identify three people who have healed some pain you felt by their healing touch.

  1. _____
  2. _____
  3. _____

- ⤍ Who in your family of origin, or your immediate family, needs your healing touch?
- ⤍ List at least three people in your place of work who need the power of a healing touch.

  1. _____
  2. _____
  3. _____

- ⤍ What Would Justice Demand of you today in terms of touching those near to you?

Remember…

I waited patiently for the Lord;
*   he inclined to me and heard my cry.*
He drew me up from the desolate pit,
*   out of the miry bog,*

Psalm 40:1-2a

My soul clings to you;
your right hand upholds me.

PSALM 63:8

Do not hesitate to visit the sick,
because for such deeds you will be loved.
In all you do, remember the end of your life,
and then you will never sin.

SIRACH 7:35-36

He reached down from on high, he took me;
he drew me out of mighty waters.

PSALM 18:16

Jesus said, ***Put your finger here and see my hands.***
Reach out your hand and put it in my side.
Do not doubt but believe.

JOHN 20:27

DO THIS IN REMEMBRANCE OF ME.

Pray...

Heavenly Father, our world has become so germ conscious it has become almost impossible to touch without having to constantly wash one's hands. We have become so litigious that it makes us nervous to reach out and touch someone, offer a helping hand, without asking permission or being concerned for a Samaritan Law.

Help me, Lord, to remember that you were the one who showed us, by your word and example, to take risks, to choose life, to be other-conscious rather than self-conscious. In breaking bread and drinking from the same cup, you left us a permanent awareness of your real presence, to help us take the risks you took to reach out and touch someone, and to do it in remembrance of you. Heavenly Father, strengthen my resolve to imitate Jesus. Amen

Pray in God's Presence

And whenever you pray, do not be like the hypocrites; for they love to stand and pray in the synagogues and at the street corners, so that they may be seen by others. Truly I tell you, they have received their reward. But whenever you pray, go into your room and shut the door and pray to your Father who is in secret; and your Father who sees in secret will reward you.

MATTHEW 6:5-6

Two men went up to the temple to pray, one a Pharisee and the other a tax collector. The Pharisee, standing by himself, was praying thus, "God, I thank you that I am not like other people: thieves, rogues, adulterers, or even like this tax collector. I fast twice a week; I give a tenth of all my income." But the tax collector, standing far off, would not even look up to heaven, but was beating his breast and saying, "God, be merciful to me, a sinner!" I tell you, this man went down to his home justified rather than the other; for all who exalt themselves will be humbled, but all who humble themselves will be exalted.

LUKE 18:10-14

Bless those who curse you, pray for those who abuse you.

LUKE 6:28

Then little children were being brought to him in order that he might lay his hands on them and pray.

MATTHEW 19:13a

In its simplest definition, prayer is about becoming conscious of and acknowledging God's presence in our lives. From that simple beginning, we work to increase our conscious awareness of God and, as in a love relationship, when we communicate better and become more aware of God, we become comfortable in the silent presence of God.

There are those who say or read prayers they have learned from childhood; there are those who sit in silent wonderment and awe of the world around them and God's presence therein; there are those compelled to write prayers, like love songs or poems, which arise within them. Some people pray with music in the background; others pray while playing a favorite instrument. Some create a sacred space and light candles; others make sacred the ground on which they walk. There are those who pray for others and seldom for themselves; and there are those who pray for miracles or just for God's will to be done. And almost all praying people experience periods of time when they cannot pray.

Prayer is like air flowing through pipes. Each pipe produces a different sound—some loud, some medium, some low—but they all make an appropriate response to the air flowing through them. So it is with us. Prayer is the Spirit of God breathing through us to God, using our individual voices, our thoughts, hopes and dreams, anger and pain, and offering all to God.

Lovers like to be alone—walking on a beach, sitting on a bench, holding hands. Their time together confirms their love for one another. Prayer does this for our relationship with God. No matter where we are, no matter what we are doing or who we are with, no one has to know we are praying (talking) to God. There is no right or wrong way to be in love. Love opens our imagination, lifts us out of ourselves, compels us to be present to the person we love.

Consider...

- ✧ What are four things you can do when you feel empty and believe you do not have the energy to pray?
- ✧ Silent meditation helps me_____.
  Sometimes burning candles and incense can_____.
  Music sets the tone for prayer by _____.

Remember...

For what other great nation has a god so near to it as the LORD our God is whenever we call to him?

DEUTERONOMY 4:7

You will pray to him, and he will hear you,
and you will pay your vows.

JOB 22:27

But as for me, my prayer is to you, O Lord.
At an acceptable time, O God,
in the abundance of your steadfast love, answer me.

PSALM 69:13a

Turn back to the Lord and forsake your sins;
pray in his presence and lessen your offense.

SIRACH 17:25

Jesus said, ***But whenever you pray, go into your room and shut the door and pray to your Father who is in secret; and your Father who sees in secret will reward you.***

MATTHEW 6:6

DO THIS IN REMEMBRANCE OF ME.

Pray…

Heavenly Father, I like to think I pray often as I offer my day to you. Yet, I am painfully aware that there are days when I am barely conscious of your presence, except for those moments when I say, "thank God," with little real awareness of it being a prayer. Holy Spirit, increase my conscious awareness of your prompting me to pray, increase my awareness of the need to pray in good times as well as bad, and help me to understand that you are still with me even when I cannot find the words to pray. Lord Jesus Christ, help me to remember your presence when two or three are gathered in your name, so that in the breaking of the bread and sharing the same cup, I make the eucharistic celebration a way of life, in remembrance of you, and not just a ritual I attend. Amen

Trust in God

*A*s he was setting out on a journey, a man ran up and knelt before him, and asked him, "Good Teacher, what must I do to inherit eternal life?" Jesus said to him, "Why do you call me good? No one is good but God alone. You know the commandments: 'You shall not murder; You shall not commit adultery; You shall not steal; You shall not bear false witness; You shall not defraud; Honor your father and mother.'" He said to him, "Teacher, I have kept all these since my youth." Jesus, looking at him, loved him and said, "You lack one thing; go, sell what you own, and give the money to the poor, and you will have treasure in heaven; then come, follow me." When he heard this, he was shocked and went away grieving, for he had many possessions.*

MARK 10:17-22

Contrary to the beliefs of some Christians, Jesus did not have a problem with wealth or wealthy people. He dined in the homes of wealthy people. Then, as now, there were those who used their God-given abilities to become materially successful. Some had an addiction to their possessions, and experienced difficulty in letting go.

The world in which we live often measures success by what we own, the size of our home, the car we drive, etc. If we cannot get past this and find inner peace, we can die spiritually, slowly suffocating from the disease of materialism.

There can be no doubt about the goodness of the rich young man. But he was unable to let go of his possessions. Unlike James and John, who left their business, boats, and partners to follow Jesus, this young man was not spiritually mature enough to take the risk.

To live freely and have choices is to lose our lives, to lose ourselves in God so that we are able to live in this world but not be controlled by it or its values. To be free is to admit our total dependence upon God; to decide to be governed by the power of love, trust, and forgiveness; and then turn our will and our life over to God. These three simple steps are the foundation for a life lived with peace of mind.

Consider…

- How do material possessions limit your ability to trust in God?
- What strong negative emotions from your childhood years continue to impact you and seriously limit your spiritual freedom?
- Who are the friends God has placed in your life to bolster your trust in God, teach you unconditional love, and help you accept forgiveness?
- Who are the people in your life that ratify material possessions are one's valid markers of success?

Remember...

Trust in the LORD forever,
* for in the LORD GOD*
* you have an everlasting rock.*

Isaiah 26:4

For thus said the LORD GOD, the Holy One of Israel:
In returning and rest you shall be saved;
* in quietness and in trust shall be your strength.*

Isaiah 30:15a

How often do we seek a geographical cure for our problems, a new job, a new residence, a new car? The movie *The Rose* makes this point when the central character believed everything would change "after Florida," but Florida never came.

Surely, because you trusted in your strongholds
* and your treasures,*
* you also shall be taken.*

Jeremiah 48:7a

Jesus says we cannot serve two masters. It is impossible to be materialistic and spiritual at the same time. Our call is to be in the world, but not of it.

Trust in the LORD with all your heart,
and do not rely on your own insight.

Proverbs 3:5

Jesus said, *Those who find their life will lose it,
and those who lose their life for my sake will find it.*

MATTHEW 10:39

DO THIS IN REMEMBRANCE OF ME.

Pray…

Heavenly Father, I am only too aware that, more often than not, my trust is grounded in that which is tangible. I have been conditioned to trust in what I know, what I see, what is firmly in my grasp. But Jesus said, "The kingdom of God is within your grasp," and I've been afraid to take the risk, to trust.

Come, Holy Spirit, and help me see the kingdom of God within me and around me. Open my eyes to see God's presence in nature; help me stop and smell the roses; let me hear you in the thunder and lightening, in the storm and in the silence.

Lord Jesus Christ, touch my eyes that I may see, hug me that I may feel, heal my brokenness that I may heal others. Help me to see that there is more to kneeling at the altar and saying "Amen" when I break bread and drink from the cup with my sisters and brothers. Lord Jesus Christ, let not this chalice pass from me, but let me eat this bread and drink from this cup, that I may imitate your life in mine, and do it in remembrance of you. Amen

Servant-Leadership

*T*hen he poured water into a basin and began to wash the disciples' feet and to wipe them with the towel that was tied around him.

JOHN 13:5

No one can serve two masters; for a slave will either hate the one and love the other, or be devoted to the one and despise the other. You cannot serve God and wealth.

MATTHEW 6:24

The kings of the Gentiles lord it over them; and those in authority over them are called benefactors. But not so with you; rather the greatest among you must become like the youngest, and the leader like one who serves.

LUKE 22:25-26

In the desert, Jesus made his decision to be a servant of God. He knew the dangers of leadership styles that lead to destruction. The power of Jesus was the power of service. In our world, the predominant image of leadership is that of power and prestige, of financial wealth and material possession. Despite that, God manages to raise up those whose moral leadership is more powerful because their strength comes from God, not from their possessions or the lack of them. These are they who want nothing but to be free to serve the poorest of the poor; they remind us that *service is the essence of leadership.*

There are three ways to view life: (1) When you help, you see life as weak; (2) When you fix, you see life as broken; (3) When you serve, you see life as a whole. Serving is the work of the soul.[8]

A patient in a psychiatric/chemical dependency hospital once asked me, "What can you tell us about ego?" I thought for a moment, and then threw it back to the patient: "What is your definition of ego?" The patient replied, "To me it means Easing God Out."

Fixing and helping may be the work of the ego: It makes us "good" to do things for others; it fills something missing within ourselves. Serving is the work of the soul. No matter how I feel, I can always reach out to help another. I can choose life, and in choosing life I imitate Jesus, dying to self in order to serve those in need.

Consider...

- ↬ How do you utilize the God-given opportunities to be a servant/leader?
- ↬ List other opportunities for servant-leadership on your part to which, at this time, you are turning a blind eye.

_____

_____

_____

_____

_____

- ↬ Give your community a careful scrutiny and ask yourself, from the point of view of servant-leadership, What Would Justice Demand from me?

Remember...

The LORD your God you shall fear; him you shall serve.

DEUTERONOMY 6:13a

Now if you are unwilling to serve the LORD choose this day whom you will serve...but as for me and my household, we will serve the LORD.

JOSHUA 24:15a-c

Jesus said, *For the Son of Man came not to be served but to serve.*

MARK 10:45a

DO THIS IN REMEMBRANCE OF ME.

Pray...

Heavenly Father, I have always thought that to be your servant I had to do something extravagant. I never considered helping my neighbor as being servant-leadership activity.

Help me, Lord God, to be more open to those opportunities you offer me daily to reach out to others, to expand on those small kindnesses that can make a difference in the life of another.

Lord Jesus Christ, thank you for showing me how to serve others, how to reach out and do those little tasks that do not draw attention to me. Thank you for showing me that in breaking bread and drinking from the cup, I can make Eucharist a way of life, and do it all in remembrance of you. Amen

Carry Your Cross

*ℐ ow large crowds were traveling with him;
and he turned and said to them, "Whoever comes to me and does not hate father
and mother, wife and children, brothers and sisters,
yes, and even life itself, cannot be my disciple."*

LUKE 14:25-26

*Then he said to them all, "If any want to become my
followers, let them deny themselves and take up their
cross daily and follow me. For those who want to save
their life will lose it, and those who lose their life for
my sake will save it."*

LUKE 9:23-24

Is Jesus going against his commandment to love one another? At first glance, this might seem so. Jesus is not telling
us to literally hate our families. Rather, he is offering us a
serious challenge to turn away from those things we hold
near and dear to us, those people, places, and things we depend upon in an unhealthy manner, so that we can become

free to serve God. Attachments can be a painful cross to carry. As a human being, Jesus was tempted to a ministry based on materialism, sensationalism, and power. He is telling us that temptation is the cross we carry in life, but the road to freedom is to die to self and serve God in those around us.

The sign of the cross, made on the forehead by many Christians, is a reminder to most of the passion, death, and resurrection of Jesus the Christ. The act of making the sign of the cross can serve as a strong reminder to die to self in imitation of Jesus. Long before his physical death, Jesus showed us how to live by dying to self. Jesus died to self and gained strength from knowing that "my food is to do the will of him who sent me" (John 4:34).

To die to our selfish wants and desires, we have to admit that, on our own, we are powerless; we have to admit we need the help of others and God; we need to admit our faults and failings and turn our will and our lives over to the care of God. It is then that we become free to serve God.

It would seem that Jesus understood the meaning of the cross, of dying to self, through his own experience and suffering, as well as from the psalms and other Scripture. He learned to turn the negative power of suffering and temptation into a power for healing, through service to God in others.

In the Lord I take refuge; how can you say to me,
  "Flee like a bird to the mountains"?

PSALM 11:1

Protect me, O God, for in you I take refuge.
I say to the Lord, "You are my Lord;

I have no good apart from you."

PSALM 16:1-2

Wash me thoroughly from my iniquity,
and cleanse me from my sin.

PSALM 51:2

My child, if you accept my words
and treasure up my commandments within you,
making your ear attentive to wisdom
and inclining your heart to understanding;
if you indeed cry out for insight,
and raise your voice for understanding;
if you seek it like silver,
and search for it as for hidden treasures—
then you will understand the fear of the LORD
and find the knowledge of God.

PROVERBS 2:1-5

Consider…

 ☙ List five temptations in your life that have to be overcome in order for you "to do justice, to love kindness, and to walk humbly with your God" (Micah 6:8b).

1. _____
2. _____
3. _____
4. _____
5. _____

∾ Which temptation do you have the greatest difficulty with in terms of letting go? How does this temptation interfere with your relationship to self, others, and God?

There are many *isms* in our society that we seem to carry lightly; we fail to recognize them as crosses. Easily and without questioning, we lift the cross of materialism, provincialism, capitalism, nationalism, classism, racism, alcoholism, etc. Our freedom lies in acknowledging the weight of each cross, in confronting it and making it personal, so that we can die to self and serve those burdened by it.

Remember…

Jesus said, *If any want to become my followers, let them deny themselves and take up their cross daily and follow me.*

LUKE 9:23

DO THIS IN REMEMBRANCE OF ME.

Pray…

Heavenly Father, daily I am tempted to turn a blind eye to the injustice around me. I am tempted to hurry past those sitting on the side of the road so I don't have to read their "Will work for food" signs. I am tempted to ignore the way employees are treated. I am tempted to turn a deaf ear to the cries of those whose silence screams for justice. I am tempted to isolate myself so I don't have to become involved, and thus to absolve myself from the world around me.

Lord Jesus Christ, I thank you for the gift of the breaking of bread and sharing the cup to remind me that we are all at the eucharistic table together, rich and poor, educated and uneducated, skilled and unskilled, employed and unemployed, employer and employee, all with our different ethnicities, genders, and sexual orientations. We all kneel and break bread together, as we will at the great banquet table on the last day. Thank you, Lord, for this gift that helps me to face the temptations and sufferings in my life, helps me to grow stronger, acknowledging my weakness and asking myself What Would Justice Demand— and then to do justice, and do it in remembrance of you. Amen

Closing Reflection

As I reflect on the life of Jesus, I see that his relationship with God, formed by reading and meditating on the (Hebrew) Scriptures, was the driving force of his life. Internalizing these, he "increased in wisdom and in years, and in divine and human favor"(Luke 2:52).

When the Pharisees complained that the disciples of Jesus plucked heads of grain to eat on the Sabbath, Jesus responded, "But if you had known what this means, 'I desire mercy and not sacrifice,' you would not have condemned the guiltless"(Matthew 12:7). Those who heard this would have understood the reference to the prophet Hosea, who said, "For I desire steadfast love and not sacrifice, the knowledge of God rather than burnt offerings" (Hosea 6:6). Jesus wanted to reconnect the people to God through mercy, love, and forgiveness, rather than through empty legalism.

Legalism focuses us on the law, not the spirit of the law, and for that reason Jesus prayed that "they may be one, as we are one" (John 17:22b). Legalism demands that we *adhere to* the law. Spirituality requires that we *know* the law; it gives us the freedom to suspend the law, when appropriate, in order to do what is right and good, for the glory of God.

Jesus never doubted his oneness with God. His life was a walking, living reality of what it means to be united with God. He was centered in his awareness God's presence, and conducted his life so as to bring this sense of unity with God to all people. That is why his followers exclaimed, "were not our hearts burning within us while he was talking to us on the road, while he was opening the scriptures to us?" (Luke 24:32).

Jesus spoke to the outcasts and the marginalized, many of whom would not be permitted to the Lord's table in some of our churches because they are divorced, have AIDS, are alcoholics or drug addicts, or simply live on the wrong side of town. Jesus touched people with leprosy, and many of us are still afraid to touch someone with AIDS. Formed by the sacred Scriptures, he made of them the cornerstone of his life: his reason for living, his guide for how to die to human selfishness and live in the Spirit of God.

As we read the Scriptures through the eyes of Jesus, our hearts too can begin to burn. We can begin to realize that these living documents call us from legalism to spirituality, from isolation to engagement, from indifference to compassion. These stories, directives, proverbs, and psalms are as much alive today as they were in Jesus' time, and they will remain alive because they deal with the essence of who we are and Whose we are. Each of us is a child of God. We belong to God, and our hearts will be restless until we return to God. We will return to God more fully alive, more fully human, if we allow God to direct our lives through compassionate relationships. We can become wounded healers to those in prison, those who are blind or deaf or homeless or naked, whether literally or spiritually.

When he saw the crowds, he had compassion for them,
because they were like sheep without a shepherd.

MATTHEW 9:36

It is easy to imagine that this concern was formed from Jesus' reading of Scripture and prayer with the psalms.

Some wandered in desert wastes,
finding no way to an inhabited town;
hungry and thirsty,
their soul fainted within them.

PSALM 107:4-5

Jesus' heart ached because legalism was killing the soul of his people. "Jerusalem, Jerusalem, the city that kills the prophets and stones those who are sent to it! How often have I desired to gather your children together as a hen gathers her brood under her wings, and you were not willing!" (Matthew 23:37). And Jesus said to his disciples, "You give them something to eat"(Mark 6:37a).

The act of breaking bread and sharing a cup is layered with meaning when seen through the eyes of Jesus. Bread begins as a seed that dies in the field to become wheat, which is crushed to become bread that is broken for us. Wine begins as a seed that dies in the field to become a vine that produces grapes, which are crushed to become our spiritual drink. As we break bread and share the cup, we remember that this action is the crossroads: We gather at the Lord's table and leave to become Church to the world; we die to self, and make God a real presence in the world around us for the glory of God, because Jesus said, *Do this in remembrance of me.*

Endnotes

1. Drewermann, Eugene. *Dying We Live.* (Maryknoll, NY: Orbis Books, 1994) 71.
2. Spong, John Shelby. *Christpower.* (Richmond, VA: Hale Publishing, 1975) 71.
3. Merton, Thomas. *Love and Living.* Edited by Naomi Burton Stone and Brother Patrick Hart. (San Diego/NY/London: Harcourt Brace Jovanovich, 1985) 22.
4. Ibid., 23.
5. Crossan, John Dominic. *A Long Way From Tipperary.* (HarperSanFrancisco, 2000) 168.
6. Nouwen, Henri J.M. *The Return of the Prodigal Son.* (NY: Doublday, 1992) 96.
7. Ibid.
8. Puchalski, Christian, MD. "End of Life Issues." A lecture given in Jefferson City, Missouri, March 2001.